MINDLESS Marsupials

Alix Wood

Gareth Stevens PUBLISHING

Please visit our website, www.garethstevens.com. For a free color catalog of all our high-quality books, call toll free 1-800-542-2595 or fax 1-877-542-2596.

Cataloging-in-Publication Data
Names: Wood, Alix.
Title: Mindless marsupials / Alix Wood.
Description: Buffalo, NY : Gareth Stevens Publishing, 2027. |
Series: Nature's worst parents | Includes glossary and index.
Identifiers: ISBN 9781482477719 (pbk.) | ISBN 9781482477726 (library bound) |
ISBN 9781482477733 (ebook)
Subjects: LCSH: Marsupials--Juvenile literature.
Classification: LCC QL737.M3 W65 2027 | DDC 599.2--dc23

Published in 2027 by
Gareth Stevens Publishing
2544 Clinton St.
Buffalo, NY 14224

Designed and written by Alix Wood

Picture Credits: all illustrations © Alix Wood;

Photo credits — cover, 5, 6, 8, 9, 10, 11, 12, 13, 14, 15, 16, 17, 18, 19, 20, 21, 22, 23 © Adobe Stock Images; 24 © Shutterstock; 26, 27, 28 © Adobe Stock Images; 30 © Les Chatfield/Creative Commons

Printed in China
CPSIA compliance information: Batch #QS27GS: For further information contact Gareth Stevens at 1-800-542-2595.

Contents

WHAT ARE MARSUPIALS AND MONOTREMES?

A marsupial is a type of mammal. Marsupials are different from other mammals because they carry their babies in a **pouch**.

What's a Mammal?
You are a mammal! Mammals breathe air, have a backbone, and have hair. The females produce milk to feed their babies.

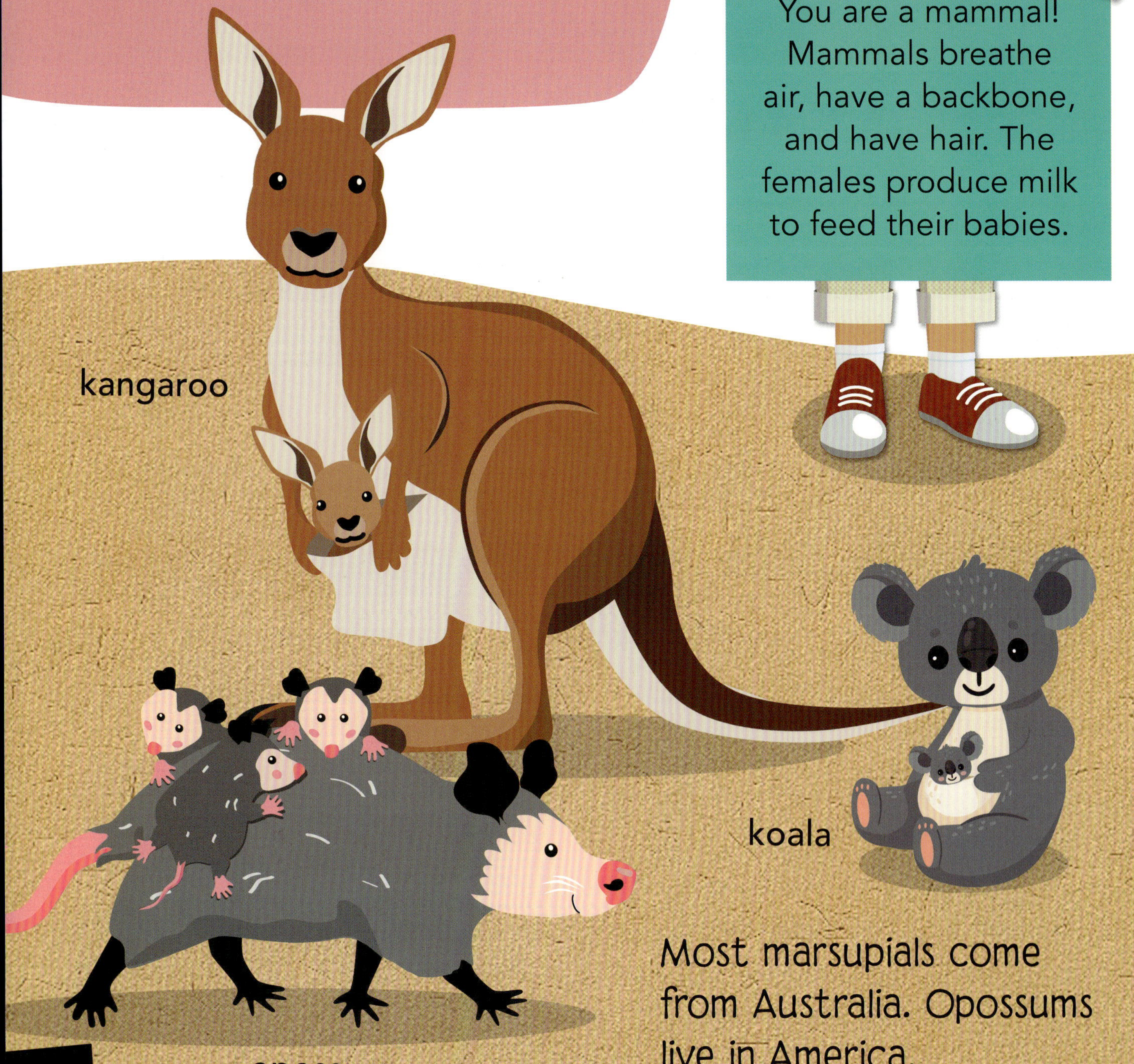

Most marsupials come from Australia. Opossums live in America.

Marsupial babies are very tiny when they are born. They crawl into their mother's pouch to drink her milk and stay safe.

a baby kangaroo in its mother's pouch

Monotremes are a type of mammal too. These unusual mammals lay eggs.

This echidna is a monotreme

Marsupials and monotremes CAN be great parents, but they also do some pretty mindless things!

Kangaroos

At around 6.5 feet (2 m) tall, kangaroos are the tallest marsupials in the world. But a newborn kangaroo is only the size of a tiny grape!

A baby kangaroo is called a joey.

The tiny joey crawls into its mother's pouch. It is too small to feed itself, so the kangaroo mother pumps milk into the joey's mouth using special muscles.

Kangaroos can bounce along at over 35 miles (56 km) per hour. Each bound can be more than the width of a volleyball court!

WHAT?

If she is chased by a **predator**, a kangaroo mom may throw her joey out of her pouch!

Why Do They Do That?

A kangaroo may have three babies to care for, all at once! She might have one in the pouch and one that has just left the pouch. She may also have another joey that is about to be born.

Throwing the pouch baby at a dingo might save herself and the two other babies!

Tasmanian Devils

Fierce little Tasmanian devil moms have between 20 and 50 babies, called imps. That's a lot to care for. So she just looks after four of them!

Tasmanian devil mothers only have room for four in their pouch. The four fastest imps that crawl into the pouch win. The rest lose and get no milk!

Why Do They Do That?

The fastest, strongest babies win the race to find food. The weaker imps won't survive. While this seems cruel, it is nature's way of making sure their species stays strong.

Tasmanian devil dads are bigger than the females.

They use their strong jaws to drag females into their den. Adult females grow tough skin around their necks to protect themselves!

WHAT?

Both males and females will eat the leftover imps!

Wombats

Wombats are strong and stocky marsupials. They weigh about the same as a Labrador Retriever.

Wombats are surprisingly fast. A charging wombat could easily knock a man off his feet!

wombat poop

Weirdly, wombat poop is cube-shaped! Wombats live in underground burrows. Scientists believe the cube shape keeps the poop from rolling into their burrow.

MY POUCH FACES THE POOP END!

So wombat joeys get a great view of the cube poop being made!

wombat joey

Why Do They Do That?

Wombats dig large burrows with their powerful feet and claws. A wombat's pouch faces backward so the flying dirt won't get in the pouch while mom is busy digging.

a wombat digging a burrow

WHAT?

Wombats have a tough area of skin on their behind. If a predator attacks, wombats run to their burrow and block the entrance with their bottom! The joey needs to hide deep in that rear-facing pouch!

Opossums

I WON'T GO BACK IF A BABY FALLS OFF!

Opossum moms give birth to tiny babies that they carry in their pouch. When the babies get too big, they hitch a ride on their mother's back.

The joeys cling on to mom's fur. They need to hang on tight!

If a baby falls off, mom may not notice. The joey will have to look after itself now!

Why Do They Do That?

Opossum moms may give birth to 20 tiny joeys. Mom's pouch only has room for 13, so only 13 of those joeys will survive. That is still a lot of babies to carry around on your back. It is easy to see why some may fall off.

If a baby falls off, it makes tiny sneezing sounds to alert mom. If she notices, she makes little clicking sounds to call them.

Koalas

Cute koalas seem like great parents. The koala mom carries her joey around in her soft, fluffy pouch. She eats all day to produce enough milk to feed her baby. But she also produces something else!

WHAT?

As the joey grows, the pouch stretches and faces backward. Now the joey can easily help itself to the gross, runny poop that oozes from their mom!

Why Do They Do That?

Koalas eat eucalyptus leaves. These toxic leaves are poisonous to most animals. Eating their mother's poop helps prepare the young koala's stomach so it can break down the toxic leaves.

Backward-facing pouches are not so great when mom climbs up a tree. Special muscles in mom's pouch tighten to keep the joey from falling out.

Once a joey is too big for the pouch, they cling on to mom's fur.

Koalas climb trees as high as a 15-story building. Then they jump from tree to tree to find the best leaves. The joey better hang on tight!

Quokkas

Quokkas are cute, smiley little marsupials that live in Australia. If a quokka mom spots a dingo, she does something that isn't at all cute. She relaxes the muscles in her pouch so the joey falls out!

Why Do They Do That?

The squealing joey distracts the dingo and gives the mother a chance to escape. If the dingo had caught the mom, it would have probably killed both of them. At least this way the mom can go on to have more joeys!

Quokkas store fat in their tails. This fat store helps them survive for a long time without food if they need to.

WHAT?

Quokkas swallow food whole. Then they throw up and eat the regurgitated food! Yuck! They do this to get more nutrients from the food.

Sugar Gliders

I'M SMALL AND CUTE, BUT I EAT BABIES!

Sugar glider moms have one or two babies at a time.

The tiny joeys crawl into the pouch and stay there for around 70 days. It can be tight in that tiny pouch!

WHAT?

If a sugar glider baby doesn't appear healthy, mom or dad will kill it and then eat the evidence!

Why Do They Do That?

There are a few reasons why sugar gliders might eat their babies. A mom that can't produce milk may kill a joey because she knows she can't feed it. A parent might be stressed or simply not have any other food. They eat dead joeys so their scent doesn't attract predators!

Sugar gliders nest in holes in the trees. Once out of the pouch, the joeys stay in the nest until they are around four months old.

Sugar gliders have flaps of skin from their wrists to their ankles. These act like parachutes. They use the flaps to glide through the air.

The poor joeys take a while to learn to glide. It's dangerous throwing yourself out of a tree! Slippery tree trunks are hard to grip too.

Common Brushtail Possum

I CHASE MY KIDS AWAY ONCE THEY ARE GROWN!

Brushtail possums live high up in the trees. Their bushy tails grip the branches to help them climb.

Newborn joeys are safe inside mom's pouch. Older joeys hide in dens high in the trees.

Sometimes joeys cling on to mom's back or tail. That can be scary! Joeys can fall off and become lost.

Brushtail possum parents do not like sharing their dens. Once the babies are grown, they get chased away.

Why Do They Do That?

Sometimes there aren't enough dens for everyone. If an area has few dens, possum moms are believed to have more sons than daughters. Why? Because male joeys travel farther to find a new territory, so they won't fight mom for her den!

Tree Kangaroos

Tree kangaroos have short, strong legs which help them climb up trees.

Why Do They Do That?

Living up in the trees means tree kangaroos can eat leaves and birds' eggs. It is not the safest place to raise a joey, however!

WHAT?

Like koalas, tree kangaroo joeys eat their mom's poop. Microbes in the poop help the joeys develop a strong, healthy gut.

Because living high in trees is dangerous, baby tree kangaroos spend a long time with their moms. A joey will stay in its mom's pouch for around 10 months. Even when the joey no longer fits in the pouch, it may still drink its mom's milk for two or three more months.

Eventually, tree kangaroo moms get tired of caring for their grown-up joeys. Moms have been seen biting a joey's feet to drive it away!

Yapoks

Yapoks live in wet areas in Central and South America. They are also known as water opossum. They nest in tunnels underground and come out after dark to hunt fish, crabs, and frogs.

I DUNK MY JOEYS UNDERWATER!

WHAT?

Yapok moms hunt in water. The moms may have up to five joeys in their pouch. So while mom is swimming, the joeys are completely under the water!

Unusually, male yapoks have a pouch too. But they don't use it for joeys. Dad's pouch acts like swimming trunks protecting parts of his body!

Why Do They Do That?

A yapok needs to hunt for food in or by the water. The adults are perfectly designed for their watery life.

Tiny, bald yapok joeys can't survive underwater.

To keep her babies dry, a ring of muscle runs around mom's rear-facing pouch opening. This keeps the pouch closed. An oily substance helps seal the pouch too.

Platypuses

Platypuses are strange looking!

> **The first scientist to examine a drawing and the skin of a platypus thought it was a hoax!**

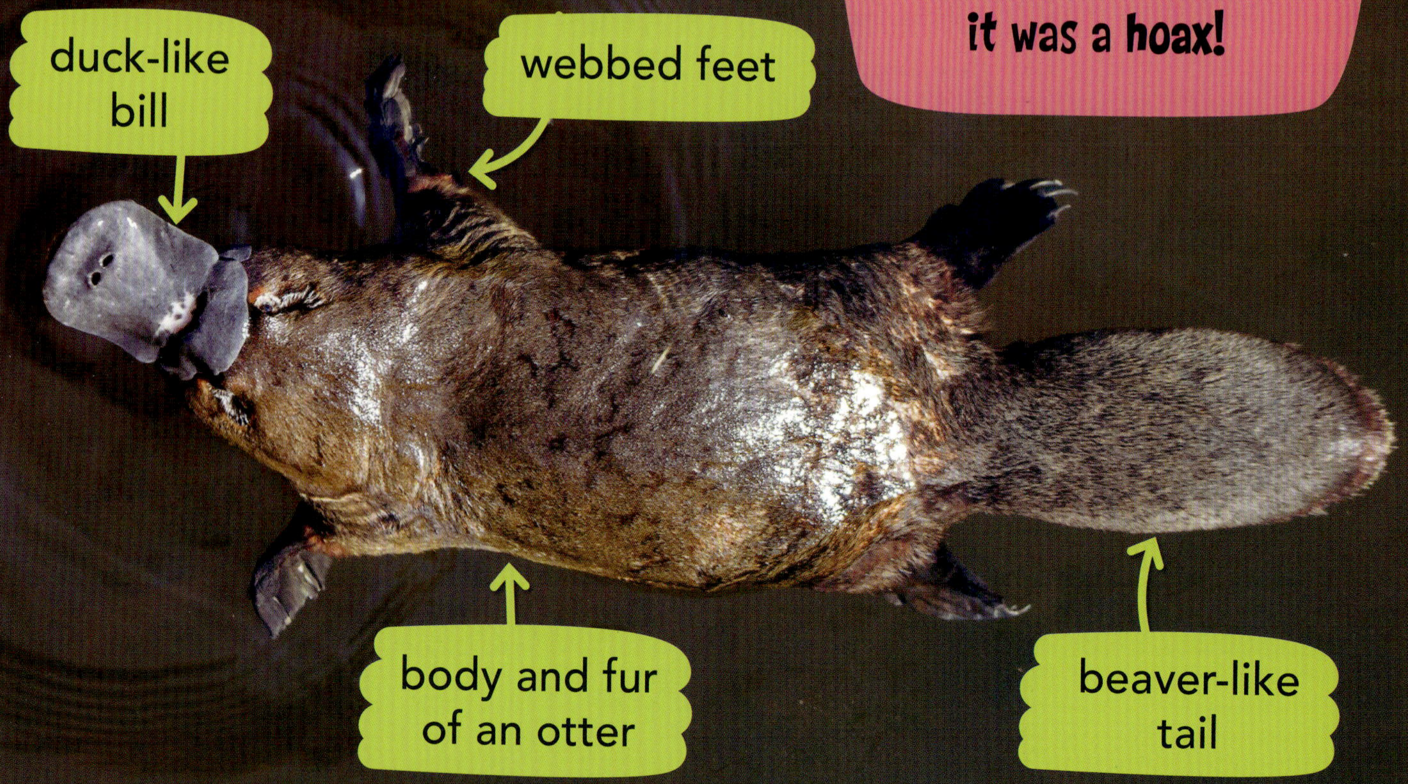

I HAVE A DENT, NOT A POUCH!

Platypuses are monotremes. The moms lay small, oval, leathery eggs in an underground burrow. Platypuses don't have a pouch. They keep their eggs warm by using their tail to hold them against a dent in their body.

Mom seals the burrow with plugs of damp soil. After around 10 days, the eggs hatch. The bald, blind young platypuses suck milk that mom sweats onto her fur.

Why Do They Do That?

Unlike other mammals and marsupials, a platypus feeds her young with milk patches covered in fur.

When the platypuses are fully grown, mom unseals the burrow. The platypuses then can leave the nest.

WHAT?

Watch out for dad! He has barbs full of poisonous venom on his back legs!

They use the venom to paralyze other platypuses when they fight each other.

Echidnas

Echidna moms lay one small, leathery egg. This monotreme mom nudges her egg into her pouch. It hatches about 10 days later.

The newly-hatched echidna uses its front legs to drag itself to mom's patches of milk.

Baby echidnas are called puggles.

Once the puggle grows its sharp spikes, it gets kicked out of the pouch.

WHEN YOU'RE GROWN, YOU'RE ON YOUR OWN!

The mom hides the spiky puggle in a burrow.

Then mom leaves the burrow for several days at a time while she looks for food.

WHAT?

At around 200 days old, mom digs the puggles out of their burrow. She feeds them one last time, and then the puggles usually never see her again!

Why Do They Do That?

Echidnas aren't social animals. They like to live alone. The only time you may see lots of echidnas together is when the males are looking for a mate.

The males will walk along behind a female echidna. They sometimes form a train of males up to 11 echidnas long!

Glossary

hoax Something false or fake presented as true or real.

microbes Living things so small they can only be seen with a microscope.

pouch A natural pocket of skin on a female marsupial that is used to hold and carry babies.

predator An animal that hunts, kills, and eats other animals for food.

regurgitated Brought back up from the stomach and out of the mouth.

species A group of similar living things that produce offspring with one another.

toxic Able to cause harm or death like a poison.

venom A poisonous substance that some animals produce and inject into their prey or enemies through a bite or sting.

Index